Rubie &

MW01172554

Book 1 - Meet the Twin Puppies!

by Nina Elmendorf-Steele

ISBN: 9781674157658
Nme's R&R Publications

Tiny Adorable Playful Inquisitive Inseparable

We're sisters, we're twins, and we're best friends!

I'm **Rubie**

And I'm **Rosie**

As soon as Nina (our 4ever human-mom) saw us, she knew the PERFECT names for us: **Rubie** and Rosie.

It's easy to tell us apart:

>**Rubie** has a **purple** collar

>Rosie has a pink collar

Sometimes, Mom calls us our names, **Rubie** and Rosie. But sometimes (just to mix us up!) she calls us Rosie and Rubie.

We've also got a BUNCH of nicknames:

>RnR,

>>The Girls,

>>>Girlie Girls and

>>>>**Rubie Dubie** and Rosie Posie.

We like having nicknames 'cuz it tells us Mom loves us and wants to keep us safe. Shhh.....Don't tell anyone, but Mom gets us mixed up ALL THE TIME!!

There were 12 puppies in our litter. 11 of us were girls. Only 1 was a boy. But we all pretty much look alike.

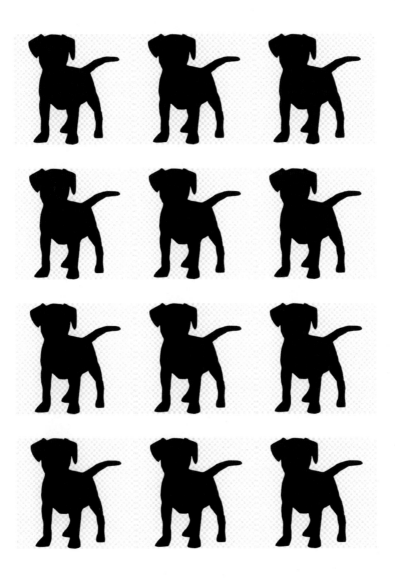

Look at all these pawprints! This is how many feet are on the sisters and brother that made up **Rubie** and **Rosie's** litter. No wonder their dog-mom and her human-mom had a difficult time caring for all of them!

So they decided the best place to take great care of all the puppies was to take them to an animal shelter. The workers there would make sure the puppies would go to great foster homes to help them grow healthy and strong.

After staying in our foster homes for 4 weeks and getting   strong and healthy, the puppies came back to the shelter. We were SO excited to see each other! The workers gave us baths, yummy food, and watched us all play together.

They took our pictures and posted online so that the WORLD could see how cute we are! That's how our 4ever-mom Nina found us. She'd been looking for puppies ever since her chocolate lab, Kopper had gone to doggie heaven. She said her home and yard were empty without dogs to play in.

When Nina saw our pictures, she called the shelter RIGHT AWAY and answered a bazillion questions. The vet gave us a checkup, our first shots, and put a microchip under our skin that helps vets know who we belong to in case we get lost. And THEN we were ready to go to our 4-ever homes!!

This is Nina, our forever Mom. We're so dog-gone cute (just look at us!) she couldn't decide which one to take, so she took BOTH OF US!! We were SO excited because now we can be best friends, sisters, AND grow up twins!

Today we weigh 7 1/2 pounds. We have brown eyes, loppy ears, otter tails, and the vet says we're mostly black labs. We have 4 white feet and white chest markings. Rosie's snout is like a lab while Rubie has a retriever nose.

Mom found this cute playpen that matches our collars. She rolls the playpen around in the house so we can see what she's doing. When it's time to sleep, Mom rolls the playpen into her bedroom and we sleep right next to her. All those things are REALLY important for bonding.

Mom wakes us up in the middle of the night to go pottie and eat a snack. But we fooled her because we're already mostly trained to go in the grass and don't need newspapers. And we're still little puppies!

Sometimes we need to stay in one room while Mom is in another. She put up a board to divide the space but we can still peek over.

We have an outside playpen too! Mom bought 4 accordion fences that can connect to make a BIG yard so we get to spend LOTS of time outside.

We like to play, eat treats, snooze in the sun, chase bugs, bark at the birds and squirrels, and roll around on the grass. And we LOVE to chew! Toys are perfect to tear apart so Mom got smart and bought us Nylabone Toys for Powerful Chewers!

After lunch, we take an afternoon nap. Rosie ALWAYS sleeps belly-up and Rubie ALWAYS sleeps on her side so she can chase rabbits in her sleep. We like it when the birds sing, the cicadas hum, or when the big toad that lives under the lilac bush makes funny 'ribbit' sounds. Talk about lazy days! We LOVE them!!

When we open our eyes, sttrreettcchh, yawn, roll over, and scratch our itches, we scurry over to see Nina, who waits so patiently for us to finish our nap. She gives us a few nibbles of a treat and then helps us practice tricks. We're learning to sit, lay, speak, wait, and shake paws. Its LOTS of fun to learn new things and we try to remember the old stuff too! And of course, the treats help!

We're eating LOTS of special puppy food to help us grow big and strong. Mom says if we squeeze out of our pen, we could get lost under the bushes in our big back yard. So Auntie Sherry made a sign for us to help us remember!

We thought Mom's garden clogs tasted SO good but then we found out they weren't food. Uh Oh! Our tummies didn't like them either so we spit them out.

Today we got new blue leashes! Aren't they cool? We're having SO much fun jumping over each other, bumping into bushes, chasing, hiding, and rolling over and over. We can run SO fast when Mom hooks our leashes to the clothesline! She says she should have called us Double and Trouble.

And now it's our first day loose on the double leash. Rubie told Rosie "Come on sis – Lets go play hide & seek! But we've got do it TOGETHER." Rosie replied, "You're crazy Rubie! It's a BIG world out there 'n I want to stay right here!

We like to stand and show off our bellies! Mom read that sometimes sister pups don't get along, so she made two pens so sometimes we can play without bothering each other. But separating us for naptime makes us howl, so back together we go. Then it's a sigh of relief as we plop down on our tummies, cuddle close, and go fast asleep.

We got invited to a birthday party at the park! We're too little to play with the kids so we just watched them and licked cake from their faces.

Sometimes we looked this way.

Sometimes we looked that way.

And sometimes we looked right at Mom.

Mom LOVES to garden and has LOTS of beautiful flowers that we're helping to pick for her — mostly because the roots taste SO yummy! "Oh No," Mom says every time she notices another flower or bush has disappeared. "You little rascals!" she exclaims and then makes us have time out because that's a No No. But those pretty things taste SO good!

We LOVE to tussle in the vege garden...

...and help pick raspberries.

Mom bought us a kiddie pool that we can splash around in. After all, we're mostly Labs and we should LOVE water! Problem is, we're kinda scared of it! So now it's the World's Largest Ever Dog Water Bowl. How cool is that?!

Then Mom decided to put sand in the kiddie pool so kids that come to play can make sand castles and roads and stuff. We're learning how to dig holes too but need a push to get into the sandbox.

Just in case you hadn't noticed before, our ears are REALLY special!

Sometimes they're flat down,

Sometimes flat up,

Sometimes right against our head, and

Sometimes 'half-cocked'.

That means our ears are on alert! That's so they can go

Forwards (when we hear a car or someone walking on the road),

Backwards (which makes us look like jets when we're running!), and

All the way up – so our ears don't get wet in the water.

AND (drum roll please!) we can change our ears from one 'style' to another faster than you can say "Zip Zappity Zoom!" Once in awhile, one ear will even go one way and the other another. How silly is that? Mom calls them our stylin' hairdo's!

Can you find our silly ears in the pictures?

Speaking of ears....

When one of us gets in a pickle, we can use our ears to help get unstuck! We found that trick worked perfectly when we were checking out what's under the deck one day. It was dark and cool and dirty – just where we love to hide!

But we got stuck and couldn't crawl out the same hole we came in 'cuz we're eating too much! We had to bark and cry until Mom heard and she came right away and rescued us.

Uh Oh!! Mom got smart and plugged the hole so we couldn't crawl under the deck anymore. But we showed her and found a different way! Only problem was, Rubie got stuck so Rosie had to use her smarts and pulled her out by tugging on her ear – very carefully! Whew, that was a close one!

We love chasing each other with a ball, running behind the couch, dashing all over the house, bashing, smashing, tumbling all over. But our favorite game is Tussle. Chaos and mayhem are full speed in this house...until Mom says 'Slow down girlie girls!'

When Mom came home from the market, we found the paper towel roll and thought it smelled like food! We ripped it apart and made a REAL MESS! When Mom found us, she laughed and said it was a good thing we're so dog-gone cute!

Guess what our most favorite activity (besides sleeping and getting tummy rubs)? We LOVE to eat!!

Mom fixes the BEST food for us, we just gobble it up! Rubie eats really fast and Rosie eats really slow, so Mom switched our big bowl for two smaller bowls. That way she makes sure we both get all we need for our bones to grow strong and our coats to stay shiny.

But that Rubie, she sneaks over and grabs some food from Rosie when Mom's not looking. So she's careful to make sure Rosie gets a lot too. Mom thinks Rubie didn't get enough food in her foster home and just can't forget about being hungry.

We just finished racing around and around our huge back yard! **Rubie** thinks she won and **Rosie** is sure she came in first. I think we'll call it a tie!

We're SO out of breath we're panting. That means we open our mouths, let our tongues hang out, and breathe in and out - in and out, really fast until our heart's don't beat so quickly. Then we lap up a lot of water and are ready to go racing again!

I wonder who will finish first this time?

Mom takes lots of pictures when we we're playing and likes this one A LOT. She said we're 'natural' models! We look and act alike in lots of ways but in other ways we're very different.

Rosie cocked her ears one way and Rubie another

We angled our heads just so cute - Mom says that's a girlie thing. And we're ALL ABOUT girlies!

You can see every one of our eight white paws and the white on our chests

You can tell who is Rubie and who is Rosie when you look at our collars: Rubie's is purple and Rosie's is pink.

This is what we look like after our scrubby-dubbie-doodle baths. Mom washes us so good we wonder if we'll still be black labs cuz the water gets really dirty.

Aren't we spic-and-span clean? We're really shiny too! Only problem is: we smell like shampoo now. So as soon as we go outside, we'll trick Mom and find some dirt or something stinky to roll in. THEN we'll smell ABSOLUTELY PERFECT!

It's time now for us to go and do some more puppy stuff – like running and eating and sleeping and playing and getting into more mischief – so that we can grow BIG and STRONG to share more pictures and stories. We're so happy that you wanted to learn all about our puppy days and hope you've had fun looking at our pictures and reading (or listening to) our stories.

Have you been able to figure out which one of us is **Rubie** and which one of us is Rosie as quick as we can bark 'Hello!'? Be sure and tell your friends all about us and see if they have heard of our adventures!

Nina is already working on our next book of adventures. Rubie & Rosie Stories - Book 2 will be available soon. Be sure to check out our social media pages for updates.

Follow us on
      FaceBook at Rubie & Rosie Stories
      Instagram at Rubie & Rosie Stories
      www.RubieRosieStories.com

We thought it would be a SUPER idea to share **10% of our profits** with an organization that works hard to take care of puppies like us and other animals in crisis.
Nina did a lot of research and decided that the Humane Society would be a great fit.

HUMANE SOCIETY INTERNATIONAL

THE **HUMANE SOCIETY** OF THE UNITED STATES

'The Humane Society International (**www.hsi.org**) works around the globe to promote the human-animal bond, protect street animals, support farm animal welfare, stop wildlife abuse, eliminate painful animal testing, respond to natural disasters and confront cruelty to animals in all of its forms.'

Made in the USA
Columbia, SC
22 December 2019